A GIFT FROM UP ABOVE

KATHLEEN BRENDA LAIRD

TRAFFORD
USA ▪ Canada ▪ UK ▪ Ireland

© Copyright 2007 Kathleen Brenda Laird.
All rights reserved. No part of this publication may be reproduced, stored in a retrieval system, or transmitted, in any form or by any means, electronic, mechanical, photocopying, recording, or otherwise, without the written prior permission of the author.

Note for Librarians: A cataloguing record for this book is available from Library and Archives Canada at www.collectionscanada.ca/amicus/index-e.html
ISBN 1-4251-0863-6

Printed in Victoria, BC, Canada. Printed on paper with minimum 30% recycled fibre.
Trafford's print shop runs on "green energy" from solar, wind and other environmentally-friendly power sources.

TRAFFORD PUBLISHING

Offices in Canada, USA, Ireland and UK

Book sales for North America and international:
Trafford Publishing, 6E–2333 Government St.,
Victoria, BC V8T 4P4 CANADA
phone 250 383 6864 (toll-free 1 888 232 4444)
fax 250 383 6804; email to orders@trafford.com

Book sales in Europe:
Trafford Publishing (UK) Limited, 9 Park End Street, 2nd Floor
Oxford, UK OX1 1HH UNITED KINGDOM
phone 44 (0)1865 722 113 (local rate 0845 230 9601)
facsimile 44 (0)1865 722 868; info.uk@trafford.com

Order online at:
trafford.com/06-2621

10 9 8 7 6 5 4

I'd like to dedicate this book,
to my husband Terry Laird,
and to our sons Matthew and
Jeremy Momney. You brought
me the wisdom, strength and
the courage, I needed to make
this book a reality, and for this I am
truly grateful. I love you, with all
my heart, mind, body and soul.
A special thank you to all my family,
friends, and to everyone who has
been touched in that special way,
each and every time they read,
any of my poems, it was you,
who gave me the little push I
needed to get this book
off the ground.

Written By:
Kathleen Brenda Laird

Acknowledgements

This book has been created by special events or little situations that have arisen throughout my life so far. These definitely have been very important, to change my life forever. You will find how touching some poems are, and how they will make you understand just how short life may be. The poems were written, with strong emotion and feelings. Like when I was happy, sad, and angry or just all and out joyful. For some people, I'm hoping it will make them realize that things happen for a reason, and just because our loved ones are not in our day to day lives, that doesn't make them forgettable. In fact the poems I have written, will keep their memories alive forever. Please understand that I have been writing poems since I was in high school. My gift was given to me from up above, it was God who gave me this gift, and for this I am truly grateful, I will use it to the best of my ability. This was how I arrived at the title "A gift from up above".

There are poems that are in memory of Jim Bratt, Stanley Momney, Charmaine Nantais, Nana, Shirley Bratt, Helen Wenger, David Laird, Lori Paskiewicz, Lynsey Dawn Chapman and a very special boy named Cody. It was you Cody that made me see, it doesn't matter just how much time we have here on earth, but more importantly how we choose to live it, and how many lives we can touch in the process. You gave me a whole new outlook on the Toronto Maple Leafs, and just how gentle even the roughest player can be, when it comes to children with cancer. You made me realize just how important it was for me to create this book and you're in my prayers always.

There is a poem written for Captain Crowley of the Windsor Fire Department, also a poem written especially for Constable John Atkinson of the Windsor Police Department. Constable John Atkinson was a true hero, who put his life on the line that day to rid our city of two drug dealing teens. For the men who put their lives on the line each and every day, we are definitely proud of you.

For you parents out there, who have had little mishaps in your life, that may not have been funny at the time, but you ended up laughing about them later, this book is also for you. I'm hoping it will make you realize that the little trivial things that happen in your teenager's lives are very real and may be traumatizing to them. Definitely don't dismiss them, help them to deal with what ever problems they will encounter. Keep an open mind and an open door policy, if ever they should need it. Should you find you cannot help, seek the professional help they require, do not feel you let them down. Try not to be judge and jury as they will have enough people to do that job. The people who touch our lives and that are no longer here will remain forever in our hearts. At the end of this book, I will put a little story I have written. It is about an angel named Pete, or spirit guide, which ever is easier for you to understand, who had spoken to my youngest child Jeremy, and just how precious God had thought his life was, to send an Angel (spirit guide) to watch over and to protect him.

    I have had several pets throughout my life so far, that have helped me through some tough times, Sparky and Chinook, who are no longer with me, but I feel they are still at my side today. The dog I had for a brief time up at Kettle Point, God sent him to me because he felt I needed the companionship and love, and took him away as fast as he came, then realizing he served his purpose at that time and I must go on without him. I never understood at that time, but I understand why now. For Taffy and Bandit who stand at my side today, and everyday with much love and without judgment.

    There will be some people, who will certainly be offended, and to those people I just have to say, that's just too bad, and thank you. It was you who put me through the tough times, which made me, write some of the poems. This is also very much needed, as a sort of therapy to get me through those days, when I felt so alone. Oh yeah, and if the truth hurts, oh well, you'll get over it, I did. You finally pushed me out of the picture; you got what you wanted, now didn't you? Now it's my turn, not for any type of revenge, as I am above that, but to let you know just how much you not only hurt me, but my family as well. At the same time, I'd like to thank you, because at that time, I didn't think my life could ever be harmonious again, but I just needed to believe, and to have faith, and today I couldn't be happier. It seems God had other plans for my life purpose, and it seems I have found it in this book.

    To my dear friend Sherry Lemmon, a heartfelt thank you, for without you my book would still be consisting of many different size papers, and very much unorganized. You know kind of like film pieces on the cutting room floors. You also helped me to grow spiritually with the introduction, and the sharing of your many powerful friends, and there will always be a place in my heart for you and your family.

To my parents, Omay and Sharon Drouillard, I would like to thank you, for all of your love and support. You tried to teach me right from wrong, you let me stumble and fall, just so I could get back up on my feet and lift my head up high. For with each and every experience, you allowed me to grow much wiser. You have had the chance, to read all of my poems, before anyone else in my life. You were definitely two critics that mattered most in my life. I thank you very much, and I want you both to know that I will always love you both very much.

Table of Contents

Pictures to Keep and Treasure 9
Wild Rice and Roses. 10
Dreams. 12
Reality. 14
A Friend In Heaven. 15
Truth or Dare 16
Firecrackers In The Sand 17
Someone Special 18
A Mother Just Like You! 20
Can't Find My Comb!. 21
Picture Frame. 22
From Eight to Six. 23
Matthew's Special Day!. 24
Jeremy's Special Day! 27
I'm Clean Enough! 29
Looking At The Remnants. 30
Family Ties 31
Something So Right 33
The Caging Of The Black Widow. 34
The Leader Of The Cult! 36
The Little Things. 37
The Flames Burned Out 39
What Is A Mother? 40
In My Heart Forever. 42
Growing UP 44
My Little Boys! 47
The Carolina's Are Not For Me 49
The Love Is There Forever!. 50
We Can't Go Back 51
I've Learned To Be A Leader 52
Ticked Off And Crazed!. 53

I'll Always Have A Friend 54
Furby Mania 55
A Lifetime With You! 56
The Union We Have Made 58
When I say I Do 59
You'll Share Your Life With Me! 61
Twinkle In Your Eyes 62
Eternal Blessings 64
Same Old Song 65
Trucking With the Grim Reaper! 66
Our Special Lucky Charm 67
Your Guiding Light 69
In Our Hearts Forever 70
Shirley You Jest? 73
With Memories There Will Be Laughter 76
The Captain 79
Someone To Watch Over You 81
You've Earned Your Wings Today! 83
Sending Love and Prayers Your Way 85
Loving Arms Encircle Me 87
The Joy of Parenting Once Shared 89
A Penny for a Memory 91
Angels on Earth 94
Glad she missed the Boat 96
An Angel Watches Over Me! 98

Pictures to Keep and Treasure

(Mother's Day 2006)

We thought we would buy you fancy pearls,
Or some type of nick knacks if you will,
Looking through the stores today,
Nothing would ever fit the bill!

For how do you get that special thing?
To show how much you care.
To thank you on this special day,
Because we know you're always there.

In combining all our thoughts and dreams,
To make all your dreams come true.
This gift lets you know how much we care,
This gift was picked for you.

So just for you on this special day,
Our love we could not measure.
For what better gift to give you,
Than pictures, you could keep and treasure.

Wild Rice and Roses

I remember when I first saw you,
And the feelings I felt of fright.
Butterflies filled my stomach,
This made me all uptight.

As I saw you standing there,
Smoking with all your friends.
If I could just walk up to you,
These feelings all would end.

Just than the bell rang,
And I knew I couldn't stay.
But could I really walk up to you,
As you were walking away.

I walked right in the music class,
My stomach all a flutter.
As soon as the teacher called my name,
Seeing you, I started to stutter.

My friends would always talk about you,
Saying you were cute.
But I kept my eyes on my music,
And played my silver flute.

Sometimes I'd see you look at me,
And wonder what you were thinking.
As for me I couldn't help but wonder,
If besides smoking, you took drugs, and went drinking.

For someone I was all dreamy eyed about,
For oh so many years.
It's really ironic that I should be the one writing this,
And fighting back the tears.

I had to walk away from you,
I couldn't let you see.
The tears that fell from my face,
As you said good-bye to me.

I keep my feelings bottled up,
It hurts not letting them out.
Still I can't really go anywhere,
For people will see me pout.

The feelings that you shared for me,
Somehow I overlooked.
It wasn't like anything I experienced,
Within any type of book.

I'll always care for you,
And cherish what we've had.
Please remember the memories,
Those were good and not so bad.

I conclude my thoughts,
With just a word of advice.
The next wedding you have,
May it be with someone you love,
Complete with roses and rice.

Dreams

I feel your body far and near,
Always by morning you disappear.
I see you in my dreams at night,
When I awake you're out of sight.
I need to feel your warm soft touch,
Because to me that means so much.
That warm soothing look in your eyes,
Is proof enough that our love won't die.
My feelings for you are confusing and strange,
Given the years I'm hoping they will change.
It really hurts to feel this way,
Really there's nothing to do or say.
I know you still love me, that's for sure,
For what I'm feeling there is no cure.
The thoughts of seeing you again,
Sends tears right down my cheek.
The lump in my throat grows larger,
Making it hard for me to speak.
The rain keeps falling from the skies,
Just like the teardrops from my eyes.
How can you go on living this way?
When all she will do is lead you astray.
The dreams I have start out this way,

I hope you understand what I'm trying to say.
If you would just come back to stay,
I doubt that I would feel this way.
I still have a long life to live,
With more than enough to offer and give.
The baby is yours but I care so much,
I know he will never be without your touch.
So please give me a chance to pray,
With our love, we will show him the way.
God is with us near and far,
He will always leave his door ajar.
If we ever need him then,
He will gladly be there like a friend.
So please understand when I try to say,
That I'll always care and need you,
In my own special way.
What would help me hurt less,
For what I know would be the best.
If I could just close the door.
And see your face in my dreams no more!

Reality

I didn't think my thoughts had varied,
Until the day that you were married.
All the triumphs and the cheers,
Were now replaced by failure and tears.

Now all I have are memories and dreams,
Nothing will work, not even my schemes.
I don't know what happened to us then,
I just know it will never happen again.

My true feelings have gradually flared,
This in turn is making me scared.
I had to know what was in store,
Now I will never have you anymore.

I'll always want you as a friend,
Until the cruel and bitter end.
So please forgive everything I've done,
Enjoy your lovely and precious son.

A Friend In Heaven

I'm feeling sorry for myself, and I have the right,
For this time I gave up without any fight.
I'm really not used to that you see,
I usually made the choices for you and me.
You told me you needed somebody then,
You couldn't even count on me as a friend.
I hope the key to heaven we both have in store,
Then once again, we'll be together to even up the score.
My little friend in heaven will help me find,
Happiness in heaven, with a clear peaceful mind.
Your little friend, I'm hoping will make you see,
That life on earth would have been much easier,
If you had been with me.

Truth or Dare

The light made your eyes so green,
Was brought right down by a moonlit beam.
I see you hair blowing in the breeze,
With the shimmer of blue from the moonlit seas.
The expressions on your face, words could not explain,
All I can say is they were anything but plain.
You're warm soothing body being so near,
Sent a liquid down from my eyes called a tear.
All I can remember are only good thoughts,
Lucky for you, that's how I was taught.
Every time I see you, our eyes lock and we stare,
It's like playing another game of truth or dare.
We both always played and I'd win the game,
Without you, it wouldn't be the same.
Only this game is real, and I lost fair and square,
So that ended a lifetime, of truth and dare.

Firecrackers In The Sand

The people had gathered to and fro,
To see where the rushing fire trucks would go.
Up the hill and to the light,
At a screeching pace caused panic and fright.
Back and forth ran the people on the walk,
With only the sound of chatter and talk.
The fire trucks came to a halt just then,
The people with shining faces watched,
As the captain yelled OK Ben.
Then up they went with colour and zing,
As the people watched and heard them sing.
Then they seen no colour and heard them sing no more,
The people than knew what was in store.
As the people left while giving the firemen a hand,
They were grateful to see firecrackers in the sand.

Someone Special

The thing you never count on,
Is the meeting of a friend.
That someone very special,
Our God will always send.

That someone very special,
That you'll have to search to find.
Someone pleasing to the eyes,
With a half decent mind.

Someone to help you through the times,
That only two can share.
That someone who when you turn around,
Will always be right there.

A friend will always hold you,
When everything seems so bad.
Someone who helps you through the times,
When you're feeling very sad.

Someone to laugh and fool around,
With each and every day.
Someone who really comforts you,
With just the right things to say.

Someone you want to be with,
For the rest of your life.
To have, to hold from this day forward,
And become his faithful wife.

I've found that someone special,
A person who is my true friend.
Someone I'll look forward to being with,
Until the very end.

In case you haven't realized,
I've written this message through.
That someone very special for me,
Can only be found in you.

Did I forget to mention too,
That with each and every day.
As my heart so quickly pounds away,
I grow more in love with you.

A Mother Just Like You!

There's something very special,
About my best friend.
She's someone I can count on,
And be with till life's end.

She helps me when I need it,
Knows when to leave me alone.
She lets me go with my friends,
When I do, gives me her phone.

She's always there to support me,
With my brother, she does the same.
Whether it's Bowling, Basketball or Soccer,
She doesn't miss a game.

When all is said and done,
There's nothing I wouldn't do.
There wouldn't be anyone more special,
Than a mother, just like you.

Can't Find My Comb!

It started out by getting up,
And went down hill from there.
I quickly took my shower,
And tried to comb my hair.

I remember having my comb,
But I don't know, when or where.
By now it was dripping,
But I could not part my hair.

Now I jelled and sprayed it,
And thought it just not fair.
That looking in the mirror,
Sticking up was still my hair.

So I wore a hat!

Picture Frame

Once there was a picture frame,
That stood eight inches high.
With budding ears, nose and teeth,
And eyes so opened wide.

Inside this funny picture frame,
A picture now was placed.
I know you would have guessed by now,
Yes, it took up Taz's face.

From Eight to Six

As I was climbing up the wall,
Just about four feet high.
A hand comes rushing down on me,
And knocked me in the eye.

I tried to run away from it,
But couldn't help but see.
The hand was getting larger,
But still coming after me.

Now I see my destiny,
A heater never dusted.
Glancing now behind me,
I realize that I am busted.

The heater was on,
So the idea I did nix.
It wasn't soon enough,
Instead of eight legs, I now have six.

Matthew's Special Day!

In less than a day,
A 10 year old you'll be,
With a WWF candle,
And with balloons taller than me.

I remember the day you were born,
Seems just like yesterday,
A fence was put together,
In a very timely way.

I got little aches and pains,
I thought I had the flu,
I never even dreamt at all,
That it was only you.

I thought I'd check the time,
To see how close the pains were coming,
I couldn't understand saying five minutes,
Why everyone was running.

Your father wanted to go swimming,
But a storm was up above,
The cover on the pool,
Was secure just like a glove.

So I sat in the trailer,
To take a load off my feet,
Uncle Dave made spaghetti sauce,
And it was time to eat.

I mentioned again,
It was five minutes or less,
Uncle Dave dropped the spoon,
Oh, what a mess.

Dad finished helping Grandpa,
To fix the back gate,
We left for the apartment,
As they went in and ate.

Your dad took a shower,
As I fed the fish and birds,
Had time to clean up the place,
And still said not a word.

My suit case by the door,
Just playing wait and see,
As he came down the stairs,
Looking as refreshed as he could be.

We got to the hospital,
With plenty of time,
Soon he walked out the door,
Quicker than a flip of a dime.

He said that he was cold,
I'm going home his words did ring,
Of course on his way back,
He stopped off at Burger King.

He did make it back,
As your head started to crown,
So in came the doctor,
With some nurses all around.

You did pop out,
As the clock reached twelve twenty,
As I swore from that day forward,
The love you would have was plenty.

So on this special day,
Not a minute will go by,
That I'll think of this special day,
Without a twinkle in my eye.

Jeremy's Special Day!

In less than twenty four hours,
An eight year old you'll be,
With WWF plates and balloons,
No more dinosaurs and trees

The day you were born,
Was an exciting day,
It was finally here,
No more false alarms they say.

It started out with a shopping trip,
So your dad could have meals ready,
Your brother came with me,
With his blanket and his teddy.

I made spaghetti sauce and pizzas,
Then put them in the freezer,
I had little contractions,
But thought they were a teaser.

I changed and bathed your brother,
As your dad came in the door,
I said he had time for supper,
But not a minute more.

We brought Matthew to Papa's,
And the hospital we did go,
We waited many hours,
Till you decided to show.

This was your special day,
At three twenty in the morning,
Your dad left to get ready for work,
Pointing to his watch and scorning.

I called your aunt just to let her know,
April 3rd was your birthday,
She said her water broke,
She would soon be on the way.

The very next morning,
Your cousin now was born,
I did know from this day on,
Your birthdays would be torn.

I know it's really hard,
Two birthdays' you will get,
I see the results of our divorce,
With acceptance, you have met.

Than there is the Taz,
With him, wrestling you sure play,
I see what best buds you have become,
What more could I now say.

You have a father and a best bud,
And this will never change,
Some people find this situation,
A little confusing and strange.

You've grown up quite a bit,
In your soon to be eight years,
One thing you must always know,
You were always loved so dear.

So on this special day,
Please forgive me if you should hear some cries,
Just like with your brother,
You bring a twinkle to my eyes.

I'm Clean Enough!

There's not much room in here,
It seems a little dark,
Maybe I should have thought twice,
Before playing in the park.

I'm trying really hard,
But still don't understand why,
They can't make up a shampoo,
That doesn't slip down in my eye.

Then they have this little bar,
That's getting kind of old,
Now that it fits in my hand,
Throw it out, is what I'm told.

I also have a wash mitt,
So I can get real clean,
It's a fuzzy little frog,
And it's funny two tone green.

It wasn't really my idea,
To go into the shower,
By now my mother's yelling,
I've been in there for an hour.

I think that now I'm clean enough,
My work in here is done,
For all the complaining I have made,
It turned out to be fun.

Looking At The Remnants

The time was getting close,
So a shopping trip I took,
Wrote down all I had to do,
In my trusty little book.

Walking through the store,
A funny feeling I sure had,
I knew the time was coming,
And I was very glad.

I come home to make some supper,
That the boys would eat,
Feeling mighty woozy,
I decided to have a seat.

Sitting down by my side,
Sipping on a coke,
My son said ever so softly,
The barbecue's full of smoke.

Looking at the remnants now,
Laughing hysterically,
We decided that KFC,
Was the perfect place to be?

Eating our supper the boys had said,
Don't take this the wrong way,
We let the chicken burn,
To have KFC today.

Family Ties

You held us when we needed you,
When we were very small,
When we tried our best at walking,
We left handprints on your wall.

You figured out just all our times,
We tried to deceive,
A firm no, and a corner seat,
We soon did receive.

You've accepted us into your family,
In a loving gentle way,
There are not enough words,
To send a special thanks your way.

We are getting a little older now,
We have to learn each day,
To accept the things that we encounter,
Upon life's little way.

Don't be thinking, that your names,
We will never say,
I'm sure something will soon come up,
And we will have a holiday.

We hope you'll have us back again,
For our love, we've surely shown,
We would hate to break the ties,
Of the family, we have grown.

A mother figure that would pick us up,
When we would slip or fall,
Along with a father figure, we would go to,
If he ever were to call.

For we've grown up with the biggest brother,
We have ever seen,
Or a singing sister with the sweetest voice,
We think is really keen.

A dancing sister that could tap,
The floorboards right back down,
With the littlest of brothers,
That could sometimes be a clown.

How many families could ever say,
How special their lives could be,
Of course no one but ours,
As you can plainly see.

Please do not forget us,
We would love to have it known,
That all the care we have shared,
Through the years, will now be shown.

Something So Right

I walked right down the isle,
And much to my surprise,
I backed right up and spun around,
Because you caught my eyes.

I reached out to touch you,
And thought it was so right,
That I would take you home with me,
And have you tonight.

I waited till we were alone,
And no sounds did I hear,
I touched and pushed so softly,
And I felt you very near.

I could never share you,
With anyone that I trusted,
When on came the lights,
At last we were busted.

When a little quiver I did feel,
Across my swollen lip,
I swore revenge on anyone,
Who took my Redi-Whip.

The Caging Of The Black Widow

I watched you from the window,
And couldn't help but see,
You pouring out your heart,
But it was not to me.

I'm sure you didn't see it,
Or didn't even know,
That you'd soon be the prey,
For this black widow.

I can't see what she's doing,
Or haven't seen it yet,
She's digging her fangs in deeper,
This I will surely bet.

It's getting even harder now,
With all the things I am feeling,
These awful mixed emotions,
Just send my senses reeling.

I know the love is there,
For this I'd never doubt,
The communications lacking,
When all we do is shout.

When you're with you're family,
It seems no one else is there,
The world could fall around you,
You would not seem to care.

I see the walls around you,
But you shut me out instead,
Of telling me what's going on,
Inside that stubborn head.

I remember the times,
When you'd share these things with me,
I'm holding onto faith,
So for now I will leave you be.

When all is said and done,
Remember who shares your life,
I've had, I've held and from this day forward,
Will always be your wife.

I'm sure you've guessed by now,
This may be a jealous rage,
I won't stop for anything,
Till the spiders in her cage.

The Leader Of The Cult!

You think your look is sexy,
Well you better think twice,
The way you dress is trashy,
And is anything but nice.

People can see through you,
No matter how you choose to hide,
Your nasty shrewd intentions,
Really, come from deep inside.

I had to walk away,
For a fight I could not see,
I hope you're proud of yourself,
You hurt more than just me.

You never gave me a chance,
Unless it would suit you,
If you didn't get your way,
A reason you found to stew.

I know the things you did to me,
Were really not your fault,
After all you had a reputation,
As the leader of the cult.

I really do feel sorry,
For the one who takes my place,
Unless she has more gull than I,
And socks you in the face.

The Little Things

It's the little things that matter most,
In our day to day life,
It's the slightest little touch or kiss,
Between a husband and a wife.

For what happens when the touching stops,
And a kiss a quick good-bye,
The laughter once shared together,
Is filled with pain and cries.

Do we try to move along,
Making tomorrow a better day,
Or do we simply cut our losses,
And good-bye is all we say.

Can you understand that simple touch,
Or maybe showing that you care,
Was what has kept me by your side,
Without the slightest truth or dare.

I didn't need your constant attention,
Or the silence of a fight,
Or those words, you know I love you,
As you rolled out of sight.

For a simple little pill,
Doesn't change the things we say,
All it did was knock me out,
To wake with a brand new day.

Still you know nothing changes,
When the sun leaves the grey sky,
And to put myself to sleep,
All I had to do was cry.

Do you understand the work to be done,
After those words "I do",
With the touching and the holding,
Fading quickly to just a few.

A little trophy figure,
I became in your life,
So should it make you wonder?
Why I'm no longer your wife?

The Flames Burned Out

It's funny how the walks we took,
Could quickly fade away,
And those special words I love you,
Became just words to say.

I'm sure you have your problems,
I know that I have mine,
I know they will work out,
We both just need some time.

With everything that we have saved,
Throughout all the years,
So trying to divide them,
With the fighting, came the tears.

The one thing that we must do,
And handle with great care,
Is to let our children know,
As parents, we'll be there.

I still would like to know,
Just how forever feels,
There's been no quick divorce,
Just many wheels and deals.

With the feeling that the flames burned out,
When we look in each other eyes,
With nothing more we could discuss,
Than how to say good-bye.

What Is A Mother?

A mother is a special person,
Who will always care,
Someone you could talk too,
Who will always be right there.

A mother wipes the tears away,
When they manage to escape,
Or puts a bandage all around,
That little messy scrape.

A mother gets right in there,
When a fights about to start,
She tries ever so gently,
To tear the two apart.

A mother gets her feathers ruffled,
When her children are in danger,
To guard against the unknown,
Or any suspicious stranger.

For a mean and nasty word,
From mothers we don't usually hear,
For a mother in every sense of the word,
Are always sweet and dear.

For a mother helps us through the times,
That sometimes could be tough,
And smoothes along the road to life,
That otherwise would be rough.

Remember without her children,
A mother she wouldn't be,
So with all our love in our hearts,
We take our hats off to thee.

In My Heart Forever

You don't know my hearts breaking,
You haven't felt it yet,
In just a week or so,
Our separations set.

I couldn't even call you,
When it was time for bed,
The lump in my throat is choking me,
And clouds fog up my head.

If this separation does not kill me,
It will make me stronger,
I'll count down the hours,
And leave you with him no longer.

He talked of the pain I'm giving him,
Because with me you'll stay,
But thinks nothing of my hurt,
When he takes you both away.

I won't use you for leverage,
This I wouldn't dare,
We'll have the best of times,
And I will show you that I care.

You don't know what it does to me,
When I read you a book,
With a smile and a thank you,
And the happy way you look.

When you close your eyes,
Simply think of me,
There's a special place in my heart,
That you will always be.

I don't know what he'll say to you,
Or could I even guess,
I know this won't be clean cut,
This divorce will be a mess.

When I'm not with you,
Please know how much I care,
If you ever need to talk,
Pick up the phone and I'll be there.

I could never leave you,
For these ties I couldn't sever,
For remember my precious boys,
You will be in my heart forever.

Growing UP

I watched you both lying side by side,
With a peaceful look on your face,
Remembering just earlier,
Kneeling by your side to say grace.

We went to your school barbecue,
And I watched you spill your juice,
I realized I should laugh with you,
And really just cut loose.

One day will come, and you'll remember,
The laughter and the song,
Instead of yelling at you,
Later realizing it was wrong.

I realized just how frustrated you get,
When things don't go your way,
Sometimes I don't always have the patience,
Or just don't know what to say.

I want you to know, how much I love you both,
And that I truly care,
Whether I am always by your side,
At home, work or anywhere.

I tried to make my words count with you,
But you do not always see,
That sometimes I have no control,
And they just have to be.

I know that you are growing up,
So really big and strong,
I realize that you'll be moving out,
It really won't be long.

You are both very different,
And I couldn't ask for more,
One day you will be equal,
And that will even the score.

Matthew you must see,
Jeremy needs to do things on his own,
We have ourselves to blame for asking you,
To take care of him as you have surely shown.

Jeremy your singing bothers Matt,
Because you're always happy.
We can only hope one day,
Your attention span will be just as snappy.

You bring out the child in both of us,
When we all play a fun game,
It's hard to realize that you have grown,
That nothing will seem the same.

As I sit here and simply stare at you,
As you are so peacefully sleeping,
I realize I am getting ahead in time,
But the memories I will always be keeping.

Lots of love forever more,
To my precious little boys,
I'm treasuring the times we've had,
With all the special joys.

So when we all look back on this,
Remember just one thing,
That in the most trying of times,
Our heart in hand we will always bring.

My Little Boys!

Will these little boys of yesterday,
grow into men today?

Will they understand what I have done,
and all I had to say?

Will they know deep in my heart,
they mean everything to me?

Will they know my heart was breaking,
when a tear from them I would see?

Will they understand not a night went by,
I didn't take a look?

Will they know when they fell fast asleep,
I removed the open book?

Will they know after I had scolded them,
I gave them both a kiss?

Will they know after the hug,
good dreams I sure did wish?

Will they know how many roles,
I have played for them for sure?

Will they know I was a nurse for them,
for the flu, I had to cure?

Will they know I was the Tooth Fairy,
who made money suddenly appear?

Will they know I was the Easter Bunny,
hopping in each year?

Will they know it was me for Santa Claus,
that found the best of toys?

Will I realize that for one day more,
they are still my little boys?

The Carolina's Are Not For Me

(Written on behalf of hurricane Floyd)

The devastation you have made,
You sure put on a show,
You've uprooted many trees,
As your speed begins to slow.

The waters slowly rising,
The roofs are all we see,
With all the media coverage,
The Carolina's are not for me.

You traveled up the coast,
You didn't stop to look,
The wreckage you have left,
Will go down in every book.

You've become a national disaster,
But we know you will be followed,
Looking at the pictures taken,
It is really hard to have swallowed.

With everything that was lost,
It's hard to fill the void,
We know that all this was made,
By no on else but Floyd.

The Love Is There Forever!

I didn't think you saw me,
I did not question why,
You were holding hands,
And looking in her eyes.

Her hair flowing gently,
In the summer breeze,
Her eyes bluer than the skies,
Deeper than the seas.

The laughter flowed along,
As quickly as a song,
The happiness was certain,
And did not seem so wrong.

If ever there was a match,
This would surely be,
The love in their eyes,
Seemed oh so right to me.

Sometimes being jealous,
Really isn't too bad,
The love grows forever more,
Between a daughter and her dad!

We Can't Go Back

Sometimes I don't understand you,
No matter how hard I try,
Your jealousy comes smashing through,
It's hard to just not cry.

There is a special place,
I go there to relax,
It's a place we went together,
And sort out all the facts.

I see the birds, trees and frogs,
And it puts me at peace,
Sometimes I just sit there,
And laugh at all the geese.

We built some special memories,
That I'll keep with me forever,
It's hard to think we can't go back,
The word you used was never.

I've Learned To Be A Leader

These tiny little specs,
That rest upon my face,
Are making me uncomfortable,
And is just a plain disgrace.

How many times,
Does it seem to be,
The words are all scrunched up,
And I need them just to see.

They aren't the best looking,
And embarrassing at that,
Since my face is round,
They make me look so fat.

Well, I could squint my eyes,
but it sure won't help me read,
I feel a little warm,
As my sweat begins to bead.

I managed to avoid the teacher,
Another time she didn't pick me,
I'm sliding down in my seat,
Just wishing I could flee.

I think it's time to grow up,
And learn to be a leader,
Hey, look the words are clear,
And now I can be a reader.

Ticked Off And Crazed!

You think this job is easy,
Well baby take a seat,
Sometimes dealing with you drivers,
Is somewhat of a treat.

Instead of you yelling,
Put yourself in our place,
There are many things we could be doing,
Than having you in our face.

We try so very hard,
To get the pars out on time,
We really don't like squawking,
And hearing it is your dime.

Think of it this way,
As if we were your wife,
Some driver started yelling,
And threatening her life.

Would that put things in perspective,
Enough to listen to us explain,
Or would you be cold hearted,
And still try to complain.

We would like to go home,
In our happy little ways,
Instead we just go home,
A little ticked off and crazed.

I'll Always Have A Friend

As I sit there thinking,
I wonder what life would be,
If ever you weren't by my side,
With your blue eyes staring back at me.

If ever I am blue,
Or it seems no one cares,
I walk out to hold you,
Because I know you will be there.

We have been together,
For a very long time,
I never have to explain,
For the actions that are mine.

I know where you are,
Morning, noon or night,
We never seem to argue,
Or have a silly fight.

You have a mind of your own,
This I'll never change,
Sometimes you just fool around,
And act a little strange.

I know you would never leave,
For my love you did hook,
I know I'll always have a friend,
In my Siberian husky named Chinook.

Furby Mania

You come in many colours,
You giggle when we play,
With your own language,
There is over 800 things to say.

When I stroke you softly,
You purr just like a cat,
With your many colours,
You look just like a rat.

You have been the rage,
This Christmas season past,
I stood in line so patiently,
And scooped you up so fast.

Looking at the children's eyes,
You excite many more than me,
With three sharp sensors,
You do more than just see.

Even when I rub your back,
You snore your cares away,
I let you sleep so quietly,
To wake again the next day.

I hear many people say,
Your name rhymes with Kirby,
By now you've probably guessed,
You're a fuzzy little furby.

A Lifetime With You!

The pain started me aching,
With every beat of my heart,
Your words were very harsh,
And felt just like a dart.

I know you didn't mean them,
And with anger you did show,
Until the tears came rolling down,
That your words began to slow.

You said you'd never hurt me,
It was bad timing at that,
With the freezing of my body,
In front of you I sat.

I couldn't believe those words,
You'd rather listen to your machine,
When with every waking moment,
Of you, I tend to dream.

Or the fact that you'd walk out,
Without telling me instead,
Or spilling out the hurt,
You had stewing in your head.

When I know deep in my heart,
That it's me you want to see,
You had every right in the world,
To say these things to me.

You had to know that I could never,
Settle for just talking,
So with hurt feelings at that time,
I decided to do some walking.

Even all throughout this time,
There wasn't a better place to be,
With your mighty python arms,
Securely wrapped around me.

With everything that happened,
I know one thing is true,
I'd be forever grateful,
To spend a lifetime with you.

The Union We Have Made

I can't believe these feelings,
I don't ever want them to end,
We started out just talking,
And wound up more than friends.

When I look in your eyes,
Our gaze is so intense,
That with this union we have made,
It definitely makes sense.

At first I didn't really know,
If these feelings were so right,
I no longer question them,
Or put up a fight.

Each an every passing day,
These feelings just get stronger,
The nights keep getting shorter,
The days keep getting longer.

One day I'll surely know,
That I will get my way,
I will never let you go,
And you will choose to stay.

When I say I Do

If I could stand on a mountain top,
To shout up to the sky,
There's so much to say about you,
Without the question why?

You make my life complete,
You leave me floating on air.
You take away my worries,
You leave me without a care.

I can't wait to make it home,
After a long hard day.
With a kiss, a hug and I miss you,
Is all you have to say.

I've never known laughter,
Until you walked into my life,
The excitement now has hit me,
I soon will be your wife.

I've done so many things,
I never thought I could,
You have never ever stopped me,
Just simply said you should.

Our friends will share this day with us,
With all the planning we have done,
For my heart that pounds so rapidly,
You definitely have one.

So on this special day,
My husband you will be,
For there will be no one stronger,
When we are joined together you'll see.

We didn't need much time,
To think this through and through,
For my love you'll always have,
When I easily say I do!

You'll Share Your Life With Me!

Standing there in front of you,
Gazing in your eyes,
It's like the angels lowered you,
From a soft cloud in the skies.

My heart keeps pounding faster,
With every word we speak,
My hands no longer steady,
My knees feel rather weak.

I've never felt so sure,
As the repeated words we say,
The clouds have rolled along,
It has become a beautiful day.

The sun shines in your eyes,
Making them as blue as above,
The tears well in our eyes,
Showing all our love.

From this day forward,
Together we will stand,
If anything goes wrong,
We will fix it hand and hand.

It seems so strange now,
With me you'll share your life,
As for from this moment on,
We'll be known as husband and wife.

Twinkle In Your Eyes

The days are getting long,
The nights don't seem to end,
It's hard to see the sunrise,
Without my best friend.

Some days have been better,
Than the day before,
Sometimes I'd like to leave,
And just walk out the door.

The angels I hear are pleasant,
At the pearly gates,
Some days I get excited,
And can hardly wait.

I hear the pain I have,
Will quickly go away,
I can't take you with me,
So for now, I choose to stay.

You have been my best friend,
For oh so many years,
I just can't think of leaving you,
With eyes all filled with tears.

So with each and every breath,
Simply think of me,
For when I finally close my eyes,
Your face is all I'll see.

You'll have my heart forever,
But no one needs to know,
I won't be here much longer,
But my love will always grow.

I'm not doing this to hurt you,
For this I hope you'll see,
That twinkle in your blue eyes,
Means everything to me.

Eternal Blessings

He gave you delicate features,
He sent you down some grace,
He gave you the gift of laughter,
To see a smile upon your face.

He gave you two great parents,
To make your house a home,
To watch you grow, and guide you,
So you will never roam.

He sent to you an angel,
To help along the way,
To watch you for all times now,
So this path you'll never stray.

He gave the gift of prayer,
So you never feel alone,
To ask for guidance and forgiveness,
'Til the day he calls you home.

Now your life will be filled with riches,
Your home, with lots of love,
As the gift of eternal blessings,
God has sent you down, from up above.

With all my love, to my Godchild
Jillian Adysen Drouillard
This 26th day of February 2006

Same Old Song

Just once I'd like for you to see,
I have feelings too.
Since you have only one son left,
I thought more time I'd spend with you.

For what kind of existence,
Am I living at this time?
Trying for your approval,
Which always seems to be declined!

I have your genes, I am smart too,
I can get things done without a fight.
It seems you can't look past my brother,
Who in your eyes was number one, right?

For when God had taken him away,
A father I sure lost.
For the cancer took my brother,
Also took my father at any cost.

You can yell at me, and ground me,
For what you think I did wrong.
In fact, my father you'll always be,
It seems that's the same old song.

If I could take back all the minutes,
Or go back years in time.
I'd give his life back to you,
Yes, for your love, I would sacrifice mine.

Trucking With the Grim Reaper!

(In memory of Jim Bratt)

I was a rugged truck driver,
As you can plainly see,
My handle was grim reaper,
I am sure you've talked to me.

I thought I'd run forever,
Nothing would slow me down,
I was diagnosed with cancer,
And still don't wear a frown.

The tasks I thought were easy,
That anyone could do,
Are getting a little harder now,
Ever to tie a shoe.

Just like as in trucking,
I have good days and bad,
No more lines at customs,
Or the brokers I have had.

Looking at this picture,
You wouldn't recognize me today,
For I've lost my greasy spoon weight,
And I've turned a little grey.

One day you may see me,
And if by chance you do,
Remember there's more to life than trucking,
You have friends and family too!

Our Special Lucky Charm

(In memory of Charmaine Nantais)

I know for your family,
Times now seem so rough,
The building of memories,
You did not make tough.

Sitting many a times,
In the crowded bingo halls,
Or the yearly vacations
Spent in old Niagara Falls.

Family memories in the making,
Of your spaghetti in their tummy,
With those long countless hours,
Sitting playing rap rummy.

We grieved for the pain,
That the cancer did make,
For the lack of acceptance,
Was just to hard to take.

For all this and more,
No more love could we see,
Still morning, noon and night,
You would sit and have a tea.

Your mother did call,
So home did you go,
We understand why,
But it still hurts us so.

You were taken to heaven,
Wrapped in angels arms,
Making their lives richer,
To have our special lucky charm.

With onion skin wings,
You rose up above,
With the smooth soaring motion,
Of the peaceful white dove.

In heaven you'll stay,
Watching all from above,
And the void in our hearts,
Will be filled with all of your love.

Your Guiding Light

(In memory of Stanley Momney)

I tried to close my eyes,
If only for tonight,
These feelings over came me,
So I had to hold on tight.

I am always with you,
Just believe and you will see
My hand is out to guide you,
Hold tight and follow me.

These words I hear more frequent,
And I want to believe them so,
But knowing I must leave you,
It's hard to just let go.

The pain I have is far to great,
For you to understand,
I've fought so much and very hard,
However, I am just a man.

Don't think for once I'd leave you,
That would hurt my pride,
I'll hold your hand and lead you,
Please let me be your guide.

So when you look up in the sky,
And see that star so bright,
Just know that I am watching,
And I'll be your guiding light.

In Our Hearts Forever

(In memory of Cody Simpson)

For anyone who has known you,
Has a special memory deep inside,
It seems in this game of life,
We're just along for the ride.

You made us see, just how precious,
Our time on earth is day by day
We should take the time for laughter;
Stop and smell the flowers along the Way.

How many children could ever say,
They have met a famous man?
One who gets paid a million or more,
For being knocked down on his can.

Just when we thought the Toronto team,
Was one of your favorite things.
You quickly piped up;
Changed your mind,
Saying now it is the wings.

Than to go one step further,
We picked Ottawa to beat.
You picked the under-dogs New Jersey,
And said Ottawa they will defeat.

We know you've met Ty Domi,
And that fancy little mouse.
You took a trip to Disneyland,
To visit Mickey's house.

You even went to Mexico,
We thought that was so cool.
While we were here shoveling snow,
You were lounging by the pool.

Even though you weren't feeling well,
you took the time to play.
you'd taught me Kirby Avalanche,
This took my breath away.

You showed us your Yu-Gi-Oh cards,
And how important some cards may be.
You shared with us your favorite movies,
For the one with Jim Carey you wanted to see.

I've heard the pain you're feeling,
Grown ups couldn't even stand.
I'm sure that God is by your side,
In fact he's taken you by the hand.

I'm sure the Angel of Mercy,
Will soon be taking you away.
you'll get your wings in heaven,
and off you'll fly to play.

I hear that up in heaven,
The pain you'll have no more.
you'll soar through the Pearly Gates,
as you knock on heavens door.

This is not the time for sadness,
As your time on earth is done.
For you're in our hearts forever,
As your new life has now begun.

With all my love,
Aunt Kathleen Laird
May 22, 2003

Shirley You Jest?

(In memory of Shirley Bratt)

We have a few ground rules up here;
That you must learn today,
The words "Mamma Mia",
Was all that she did say?

Well, while we're on the subject,
I have, some of my own,
If we compromise on just a few,
I'll try to watch my tone.

I'd like my morning coffee,
To continue all daylong,
With an endless supply of cigarettes,
With that you won't go wrong.

We'll have spaghetti on Wednesdays;
They say that mines the best,
T.V. to watch my favorite shows,
If I decide to stop to rest.

I could hardly wait for the cards,
To play my favorite game,
With some family here we'd teach you,
Rap rummy's the name of the game.

Before we go much further,
Your life we must review,
After mom died, raising Basil & Betty,
You tried to start a new.

You were definitely a trucker's wife,
This started out, as so much fun,
Than came Jimmy, Jan and Jeffrey,
Your son's hearts you sure have won.

You'd stay up to watch hockey,
Just to hear the score,
Than tell Jeff in the morning,
Before he walked out the door.

You were Gram to everyone,
with a special heart of gold.
With a knack for being feisty,
This kept you from getting old.

Your friends loved to visit,
And for a rib dinner you would go,
Mary Anne, Winnie, Gail and Anne,
You were glad when they would show.

The girls you'd make feel special,
always calling them baby doll,
Then lending an ear for any problem,
Should anyone just call?

You called any animal little peanut,
if they were sure to stop.
For your special cat Tiger,
No animal could ever top.

In heaven; there will be no judgment,
for with the angels you will stay.
God has taken your earthly pains,
You are now free from them today.

You'll be thought about each morning,
they'll cry for you each night,
your memories live on in pictures,
You'll be their guiding light.

What you are to do right now,
is to watch from here above.
Soon the babies born unto your family,
Will now be sent, with all your love.

In completing now your destiny,
No, a sandwich is not your quest,
you're really stuck on this coffee thing,
Shirley you jest! "Mamma Mia"

With Memories There Will Be Laughter

(In memory of Basil Di Gianfelice)

It sounds like when you were younger,
You had a lot of spunk,
You took Betty and friends to a drive in,
But you stuffed them in the trunk.

You used to go with the gang,
To the Hi-Ho in your younger years,
To fill up on malts and burgers,
Maybe a few root beers.

There was a memory of you at Chrysler;
Getting tickets for all to go,
Across the Amherstburg ferry,
For a fun filled day at Boblo.

Your memories are still here,
For they are not a hazy fog,
Like going to Belle River Beach,
For the quarter foot long hot dog.

You were also a Big Brother,
You gave more with no neglect,
Well to go one step further,
You treated all with respect.

You loved to work on cars,
You're thought that work was the best,
You were caught painting with a roller,
Before you stopped to rest.

You went to Bingo halls,
Just to have some fun,
Maybe you went off to the casino,
Hoping this day was the one.

With all that you have been through,
The hardships and the strife,
For in you later years,
Religion became a big part of your life.

When you got a little older,
a trip for a new home you did take.
To stir up lots of laughter,
With many friends to make.

When you were asked to do this,
you replied "yes, I can".
little did we know in time,
You'd become a real ladies man.

It was again to our surprise,
you would do another thing.
The ladies quickly turned around,
And simply crowned you King!

If they say laughter's the best medicine,
You should have been just fine.
But life on earth is precious,
As we live on borrowed time.

So should we be so selfish,
to want to keep you here on earth,
God has all the power,
He has taken you for what your worth.

Now the angels need the laughter,
our hearts with so much sorrow.
But the memories left from you,
Will take us through tomorrow.

Now the angels need the laughter,
On fluffy clouds you will pray.
The earthly pain you'll feel no more,
For in heaven you will stay.

As I wrote this poem to you,
I couldn't think of a word to say.
so I prayed for you Basil, to God,
To give me these words today.

The Captain

(In memory of Mr. Crowley)

It's hard to close my eyes to sleep,
Knowing your all alone,
For you cannot call to talk to him,
By picking up the phone.

You have so many memories,
Those are the building blocks of life,
With the people that he's helped so much,
I'm sure you were proud to be his wife.

With the stories that I heard,
As I was walking though the hall,
He built a solid foundation,
And was an inspiration to all.

With the title of Captain,
He had to be the best,
For the ones that truly loved him,
Knew he was admired by the rest.

For what fills this so called void,
That his love for the job has made,
We go on wishing ever more,
That for one more day he stayed.

I guess God needed a captain,
But not to fight fires,
From above watch down on his crew,
And be considered semi-retired.

We need to remember all the good things,
He's accomplished in his life,
Pass on our prayers and sympathy,
To his children and his wife.

Someone To Watch Over You

I didn't think you'd walk away,
I thought I truly failed
You packed up all your room,
And to your dad's you did bail.

You left us all wondering,
Just how long it would be,
But never coming home again,
We didn't think we'd see.

I see you on holidays,
And special occasions in the making,
For any other days,
You never think of partaking.

Instead of my birthday,
A retreat you did go,
I tried to understand,
But my feelings sure did show.

Now you are sixteen,
You can drive and get a job,
But your younger youthful years,
I feel I have been robbed.

You're truly growing up,
One day I hope to see,
A charming strapping young man,
Staring back at me.

Now you want to join the reserves,
Your decision I respect,
I hope this is something you want,
And not saying what the heck.

I can't take you for your license,
Just like I truly planned,
By moving to your dad's now,
He has the upper hand.

You've always had a level head,
So I see you're growing up,
Some how I feel a little gypped,
Like half an empty cup.

I pray for someone to watch over you,
Now you don't want me there,
That one day you'll look back,
And know each day I truly cared.

You've Earned Your Wings Today!

(In memory of John Atkinson May 9, 2006)

My life purpose I have filled,
As God has taken me today,
Please don't be too sad for me,
Just bow your heads and pray.

I may not be around now,
To share in day to day life,
Remember, my legacy will live on,
In my children and my wife.

So keep me in daily conversations,
Joke around with me any chance you can,
For my spirit will be with you,
To guide and hold your hand.

Many tearful eyes around us,
Not even another good-bye,
Too many questions left unanswered,
The first we ask, Lord why?

For in the tree of life,
Many branches do we make,
God gave us seeds to start the first,
But a branch we should never break.

So don't be too sad for me,
For my new life has begun,
Let the angels comfort and guide you,
To feel better with the rising sun.

There are two more punks off the street,
That will sell to kids no more,
For I've helped make the streets a little safer,
Than the day before.

I guess the good that I have done,
Has earned my wings today,
I've done all I was supposed to do,
Now I must be on my way.

For each day will get much easier,
That the one before,
I'll take your pain away day by day,
Until you have no more.

I now will serve a higher court,
For this, you can bet to be true,
I'll still be there for all of you,
I just won't be one of the boys in blue.

One day your heart will stop aching,
You won't quiver when you speak my name,
You will cherish the life we shared together,
You're right, life will never be the same.

Sending Love and Prayers Your Way

In Memory of David Laird and Lori Paskiewicz
October 2, 2006

What happened to those days,
When we went camping and to the beach?
No one realized at the time,
The lessons we'd soon teach.

The pictures of us fishing,
For the biggest catch of all
Spending time in the Bay,
Until our parents were to call.

For it doesn't seem right,
A parent out live their child in years.
To go one step further, losing two in a week,
There are just not enough tears.

For losing a fine son,
When he came back home to stay.
Than to lose his sister a week later,
What could a mother say?

We didn't spend much time together,
We grew apart as we got older.
In reminiscing on this day,
With pictures in a folder.

I didn't know you had come back,
Or I would have dropped in on you.
For what little time we didn't have,
If only we both knew.

I know you both can hear me,
As I talk to dad a lot.
I'm sending love and prayers your way,
I thought I'd give it a shot.

I'm looking into a different regimen,
I think I'll change the way things are done.
For I can't see not being around in years,
To watch my children have their sons.

Loving Arms Encircle Me

(To help guide Tristan Chapman)
October 2, 2006

I have every right to be angry,
You didn't seem to care.
I asked you for help and guidance,
It didn't seem like you were there.

So should it be any wonder,
Why we lose faith at all.
When we plead to hear your answers,
But seem to never get your call.

How could you take a mother?
Leaving her child from the start.
What could have you been thinking?
Do you even have a heart?

I'm sorry, if I've doubted you,
Someone special you must have needed.
For reading your words in red dear Lord,
Your words, I've never heeded.

I surely do feel better now,
Three months they sure have shared.
How could I have ever said dear Lord?
That I didn't think you cared.

For when I took a deep breath,
And thanked you for your time.
Stopping to realize for this minute now,
It was you, helping me with this rhyme.

The weight has now been lifted,
With the understanding why.
I felt loving arms encircle me,
When I bowed my head to cry.

Please look over this dear little one,
With the love I know you'll send.
With Angels all around him now,
Let him know you'll be his friend.

The Joy of Parenting Once Shared

(In memory of Lynsey Chapman)
October 2, 2006

I know your heart is broken,
For many it feels the same.
Don't be afraid to talk about her,
Don't be afraid to speak her name.

The memories you have to look back on,
The joy of parenting once shared.
The mixed feelings you shared together,
In knowing she always cared.

Get mad right now if you have to,
Cry yourself to sleep today.
Just ask her for her help, to guide you,
To simply show you the way.

For part of her still lives on,
In the life she helped to make.
Should you feel you can't go on,
Look in Tristan's eyes, for goodness sake.

Never think you are alone,
Just pray and God will be there.
To comfort and to guide you,
To help carry this cross you bear.

So tell that precious son of yours,
Just how special his mother was to everyone.
Make him understand what his life meant to her,
To spend a little time with her son.

You must look on the bright side, of this life's lesson,
God could have taken her the day he was born.
It wasn't her time to go to heaven then,
And your life would have surely been torn.

She'll be there for his first words,
For the very first steps he takes.
She'll be there for all his birthdays,
To watch you bake the cakes.

Please remember all the time spent together,
At Baseball, Bowling, or a stroll in the dark.
Bring the words she wrote on paper,
When you take a quiet walk in the park.

So don't ever think she missed these things,
For all the firsts in your child's life today.
Just feel her presence all around,
Include her in everything you do or say.

A calming feeling will come over you,
To let you know you're not alone.
For one day you will be together again,
When God chooses to call you home.

A Penny for a Memory

(August 26, 2006)

I remember oh so vividly,
The porcelain fireman's head.
Going into the kitchen,
By Uncle Walter we were lead.

We would now put in our hand,
To see what we'd pick up.
By making our hand grab,
What ever we could cup.

My hand is getting bigger now,
I heard my brother say.
Pennies by the handful,
How much could I grab today.

Then there was the back yard,
Flowers and fruit as far as the eye could see.
Never afraid like today,
Of the special honey bees.

Then over to the rain barrel,
To give the plants a drink.
Not in our wildest dream,
Extinction would we ever think.

Then down through the basement,
Cucumber washing I recall.
That soon turned into pickles,
Not a job I minded at all.

Then up the stairs to the kitchen,
We would have some fun.
To stuff the cucumbers in the jar,
Pushing them in one by one.

My Aunt Frances was the greatest,
And boy could she ever bake.
It was never any struggle,
To eat her short bread or cheesecake.

Then there was Uncle Walter,
In which football was his game.
Eating poppycock and relaxing,
Was now to be his fame.

One day we took a car ride,
Off to his work, at school.
So he could dump some chlorine,
Into Riverside High School's pool.

Back to the house, up another flight of stairs,
Was my Baba's home.
She had everything she needed,
So she didn't have to roam.

Still until this very day,
Baba's honey cake I cannot make.
Hers turned out three inches high,
Now that's what I call a cake.

She taught us Ukrainian Easter eggs,
Even before we learned to write.
As I think about it now,
I'm sorry I put up any fight.

Every day I thank God for Baba,
For this gift that I was shown.
I still practice 'till this day,
But my eggs are still not blown.

I cannot see messing up the design,
To put a pin hole in the ends.
For if I crack the shell,
This I cannot mend.

Now each day it seems my back yard,
Today more beautiful than before.
Thanks to my caring relatives,
I couldn't ask for more.

I never realized until now,
This is my heaven on earth.
Now counting all my blessings,
At my Auntie's new re-birth.

Angels on Earth

(August 18, 2006)

My heart was clearly broken,
In every edge there was a tear.
My fish lay in a bucket,
For this I could not bare.

We struggled for several years now,
We made this pond, our heaven on earth.
Entrusted with Gods live stock,
We're granted more fish by birth.

We didn't have to name them,
For each fish different markings you know.
Taught them to come when we were calling,
Much affection we sure did show.

Our plants lay on the ground now,
The other pool you did not fill.
I could not bear the thought alone,
That this would be truly Gods will.

How could this happen to us,
For the ache seems far too great.
Could you not have called another?
Instead you choose, our fish, their fate.

If it wasn't for having friends now,
We don't know what we would have done.
In our hearts were truly grateful now,
Our respect they have surely won.

Now I understand why now,
God says it's better to give then to receive.
One day the tables may be turned around,
In your heart, you'll just have to believe.

What angels brought you to us?
Were we granted now our wish?
What greater gift to be given,
Than to be entrusted, with some of your fish.

There are no words to be spoken,
The healing process is all but done.
If ever there were Angels on earth,
You would definitely be the ones!

I guess a lesson's too be learned now,
With the pond there was never any haste.
Not enough time given to friends and family,
So again, there was just as much waste.

We will always count our blessings,
For each day we'll start a new.
We will be grateful for the new found friendship,
That we have found in you.

A special thank you goes out to Collin and his family.
Written by Kathleen

Glad she missed the Boat

My Baba came to Canada,
When she was 9 years old.
Then shipped back to Ukraine,
At 15 she was told.

Unless of course you marry,
That makes everything alright.
We will then leave you here,
And depart without a fight.

At 15 she was married,
In Winnipeg I was told.
To a boy named Peter Wenger,
This somehow seems so cold.

In 1912 went to see her parents,
For a vacation she did go.
As for now she was with child,
And her belly sure did show.

Her father said she should leave,
Before the war broke out.
For fear this was the last ship,
Leaving port with out a doubt.

So her name was on the roster,
On the Titanic she would sail.
Did the Lord have full intentions,
For her plan to somehow fail?

She was devastated but than her son,
Was soon to now be born.
After having Uncle Walter,
Leaving home she was now torn.

There was another ship leaving,
This she thought so keen.
As the war would now break out,
The year was 1914.

In Canada in 1917,
To a daughter now gave birth.
This made her ever grateful,
And gave her new found worth.

In 1918 the war soon ended,
But really not to gloat.
It's funny you hear this in jokes,
But I'm glad she missed the boat.

An Angel Watches Over Me!

As I awoke with the weekend sun peering into the bedroom, I could hear a one sided conversation taking place in the front room. I tip toed ever so softly, to keep the creaking boards in the kitchen to a minimum. As I slowly approached the doorway to the front room very quietly, I could still hear Jeremy talking. Still unaware of my presence, he continued with their conversation. I asked Jeremy, "Who are your talking to?" As if I could see this person too, he pointed and said, "why Pete of course Mommy." Just then chills went up my spine, then a calming feeling came over me. I then asked, "Who is Pete?" Jeremy replied, "Can't you see him, he's right there mom." I said, "Why no I can't" still puzzled and very unaware, of what the situation was unravelling to be. Then Jeremy proceeded to tell me that Pete started to talk to him first. Still somewhat skeptical, I asked, "and just what did Pete have to say?" With anticipation and excitement, I listened to his story. "Well" he said, "Pete had a wife, and four children." he continued to tell me Pete's story, I then asked what happened to them? Jeremy explained, "That they were burned in a house fire, but they are all fine in heaven now." As those same chills came back, I decided it was time to sit down and listen to the story, as I could feel the colour now draining from my face, and now feeling a little light headed. The conversation continued with the type of house Pete had, what kind of car he drove, right down to the make and model, year and colour, and the detail as to what was under the hood. That's when it finally hit me, there is no possible way, he could have ever known about that type of car, as he was only four going on five years old at the time, and no one has ever owned one in our family. I then asked, "Why is Pete talking to you?" the answer I received would make any mother defensive, "Pete is my friend, and he said he would tell me when the time was right." I snapped back, "What do you mean when the time was right?" My son ever so calmly said, "Don't worry mom, Pete says everything is going to be fine, and he wouldn't let anything happen to me." I guess just than a wave of relief come over me, and for the next two days, I listened to the tales from Jeremy, that his new found friend Pete had told him. On the third day, I had a not so right feeling all day long, and as I put both Jeremy and Matthew to bed, we said our prayers. Jeremy said,

"Pete likes that" and hopped right into bed. As I finally drifted off to sleep, I could hear some shuffling upstairs, I got out of bed as quickly as I could, only to find Jeremy at the top of the stairs trying to get dressed, having a hard time inhaling, even the smallest of breaths. I then said "I will get your puffer," Jeremy came back with, "There is no time, Pete says I have to go to the hospital right now." Without any question or a doubt, I scooped him up in my arms, and drove him to the hospital. As I walked into the emergency ward the guard looked at me, and I said, "He can't breathe." He rushed us past the triage nurse and brought us right into a room. Within minutes they had Jeremy hooked up with a mask filled with ventolin and oxygen. As I watched and prayed, Jeremy said, "you see mom, Pete said there would be nothing to worry about, and that he would take care of me." The only words that had escaped my lips, were, "Thank God for Pete." It was after that, that we didn't hear anymore of Pete. I guess we all have a guardian angel around us, and they are there when we need them the most.

You see adults; have a hard time believing, in what they cannot see. Children, being so pure at heart, and so innocent, can and will hear and see things we as adults choose to ignore.

ISBN 1425108637-6